younger
KIANA LIN

Younger copyright ©2022 Kiana Lin.

All rights reserved. No part of this book may be used or reproduced in any manner whatsoever without the written permission of the author, save in the context of excerpts for reviews or education.

ISBN: 978-1-7363255-8-2

Written, edited, and produced by Kiana Lin.

Cover design by Kiana Lin.

www.creativeinklin.com

You knew who you were.
You knew what you needed.
Thank you for that surety.

SOWN

Younger than tomorrow,
More innocent than
We will ever be again.
And, yet, already the seeds
Of our faults have begun
To be sown.

Heart just beginning to pump,
That first taste of air
Still miles away,
And—even then—
I was thought to be something
Unusual,
Abnormal,
Rare.
Already, I was loved, gifted,
Allowed the chance
To prove her right.
I was different from the start.

Names have power.
From my first breath,
I was known, called:
Season's beginning,
Gatekeeper of purity,
Goddess of the moon and the hunt,
My love,
Great mountain–
With such destinies contained in mere letters,
Such visions shaped and formed in words,
Such history flowing through my veins,
Who could I become?

It's not how remembering works,
Not really—
Or so they say.
But when my existence
Is already atypical,
Why wouldn't my memories
Be unusual too?

My first memory is of flying–
Night, stars, and clouds.
Is it any wonder my mind grasped so tightly?
That adventure and freedom,
Darkness and the unknown,
Have always called me so keenly?

Searching,
Seeking,
Savoring
Any chance to ask questions–
To find the pieces
Of my missing self.

Eccentric, they called me,
When nothing else would fit.
Dressing room curtains closed
On the tailor made pieces
Just out of sight.

I was wild,
Once.
Wind-tangled hair,
Sun-darkened skin,
And wonderingly large eyes.
Gangly limbs and crooked teeth and outrageous words.
I had never met a stranger.
I knew heat only from the sun
And the warming love of a large family.
I thought fast and talked faster and dug in my heels.
I stood my ground without effort–
If only I could have stayed that way.

I was at a time in my life
That most observers might have called my happiest.
I was uninhibited to the naked eye.
I had giggles and tantrums.
I was well-loved,
Well fed,
Well intentioned.
But what lay deeper,
Further than even I could reach
At such tender years,
Was hurt and reality that was beyond
My inexperienced comprehension.

Enjoy the moments of bliss,
The wonder and warmth
Of exploration and love and play.
The feelings of fullness,
In the midst of my young oblivion
And brimming home–
They will not be found again
For years to come.

Not sure what happened–
I changed, seemingly overnight.
I was no longer untamed.
I thought faster and talked slower,
Measuring everything I said and did.
The world was full of strangers with expectations
That I could not begin to imagine.
And the imagining was what haunted me:
A looming shadow
In an otherwise shining young life.

It is, admittedly,
Strange.
I gaze into the unknown,
The gaping dark
Of responsibilities,
Expectations,
Life–
And all I feel
Is a disjointed
Numbness.
Could I even see
That far
To begin with?
But place me before
Endless
Seen and known
Possibilities,
And I am flooded,
Overwhelmed,
And paralyzed
By the littlest,
The easiest,
Things.

Quiet voice, sharp tongue,
Watchful eyes, rampant mind–
Learning to camouflage already.
When I was allowed to dress myself,
The only things I choose to wear were costumes,
Clothing meant to disguise.
Even then,
Hiding behind my own face,
Using someone else's words.

Simple framework,
Sturdy materials–
Still,
It seems too little
To keep out the monsters,
Too fragile to keep them in too.

Perhaps I was some other creature, not quite a monster,
But close.
I looked human, but I felt so much,
Too much.
I was hungry, starving for just a bit more
Of everything.
I learned and adapted to keep everyone out: There was something
To prove.
That something was unknown, seemingly unreachable,
but–
Only just.

A carefully laid line
Leading to the dynamite that
Inevitably exploded in my mind.
The key I had been missing
Was working the tumblers,
Until everything just clicked.
Behind the door lay everything I could want–
More than I could imagine desiring.

Worlds I could not fathom,
Magic in my hands.
So very young
And I knew the intricacies
Of immortal minds–
Could hardly sleep
With the knowledge
That more lay
Just beyond the
Next page,
The last
Word.

It may sound easy
To let nostalgia lead,
But–
The old fairytales
Sometimes can't help,
Are changed and different,
Even now.

It's just fiction,
You tell me—
As if I couldn't recognize
My own hurts
In this fantasy.
And my grief
Knows these grooves
Too intimately
To not slot
Right back into its place.

I watch television
With you
Because no one
Would read my books
With me.

It's 1:00 AM
And you've been slumbering
For ages.
It's 1:01 AM
And I'm not sure I will ever sleep
In eons.

Loneliness, too, begets beauty.

Never mind that melancholy and angst
Were always my closest friends.
Never mind my love of wandering
In the dark and quiet and late hours.
After all–
Liminal beings can never be minded.

Heartbreak comes, even so young.
I did not understand,
I did not comprehend.
They tried to prepare me, but I never believed.
I wasted my days with the familiar
Until there was only one left.
When the realization and the hurt
Stabbed sharply into my mind and heart
The only consolation was time–
The very thing *drip, drip, dripping* away.

The grime accumulates
Daily,
Even without
Seeming cause or
Notice.
Windows, so often,
Need washing–
A thorough scrub
To make things
Clear.
Of course,
It's why we have
Tears.

A beat too fast,
A step too slow,
A twirl instead of a dip,
A spin out of control–
A dance I could never understand,
A trip that was always coming.

I was never quite as oblivious
As I must have seemed.
I saw more, felt more,
Than anyone gave me credit for–
More credit than I gave myself.

When a single person is a world,
You may think your view has shrunk,
But–with a universe contained in flesh–
Your galaxies are yet to be explored.

I wanted to forget,
To be far away from there.
I wanted to explore, to learn,
To not be limited by the word, *No.*
I made it to the portal,
Foot just phasing through,
Before I was stopped,
Caught between two realities
By my strongest tether.
So I turned back,
Unpacking all that I had prepared.
I wanted to forget–
I was made to remember.

Yet all was not lost.
I may have been a shadow of my past brightness,
But I channeled even that into something
Beautiful, restful, peaceful.
If I was to be a shade,
At least I would be a shelter.

No one understands me, my restraint.
How I, once so wild and fiery
Myself,
Can possibly be so calm, shedding silent tears–
So resilient against, patient with, the rage in
Her.
I am begged to strike back, to bite,
To claw and howl, to stand up for my own
Benefit.
But maybe my stillness can help,
If used for good, maybe it won't feel like
Lying.

Trapped, caged, leashed:
Why does that feeling, the sense of it,
Haunt me so?
Binds of my own making,
Tying myself up tighter than even my tangling fingers
Could manage–
How to gain their notice
When I had gagged myself so thoroughly?

Pain I didn't even notice
Welling up inside,
Welling up without
Preamble.

The past I can now see
For what it was,
For what it never was
Afterward.

Our greatest loves
So quickly become
Our worst fears.
What once brought joy
Morphs into terrors
More haunting for
All their intimate
Familiarity.

Oddly, the people
Who drive you insane
Are the ones who never
Meant to do so.

It's not that I didn't waver,
It's that I couldn't.
Incapability
At the base of a person
They thought so very
Competent.

According to you,
I am comprised of
Too many halves
That never made a whole.

How long did we share secrets,
Getting to know ourselves
By delving into deep conversations?
How many years did I spend by your side,
Watching you lie to yourself?
How many more, before we finally met you again?

Was I just so good at hiding,
Or were you never even looking?

My peculiarities you called
Bright.
My intricacies you named
Gifted.
Myself you labeled
Golden.
My discomfort and yours,
Undiagnosed.

The backtrack or the prerequisite—
Which will hurt less?

Sat in the dark,
And it's too bright
Behind closed eyes.
Alone and yet not,
Silence blaring,
Still, but every inch vibrates–
What to do with yourself
When the mind and brain
Are at war?

The colors are still there,
Though muted–
They don't just cease to exist.
They simply go unappreciated,
Awash in a light that blinds.

Content in unhappiness–
The curse or the cure?

Life was not all gloom and darkness.
There was light and laughter and growth,
Always shimmering through.
Because contentment and simplicity
Are my greatest superpowers.

I can handle your worst,
Those things you say,
The hurts you toss about.
What is beyond me–
What is true torture–
Is the hovering,
The looming,
The impending,
The inevitable.
What kills is the wait,
The weight of
Your expectation.

All the world is impossible
At the edge.
The whole universe is at hand
In the suspense.
Freedom is never closer than
On the descent.

Impossible to miss now—
The crevices that became
   Our canyons.

Defining moments,
The way of childhood:
When fallible memory
Meets
Visceral, lasting feelings.

How sad,
That sometimes
The kindest thing
Is to abandon all
And be kind
First to oneself.

Older, as time goes by,
With fewer stars in our eyes.
But–for now–
We have unexplored galaxies
Brushing our fingertips.

Young,
They tell me—
I look so
Young.
But the only thing
I no longer feel,
Haven't for so long, is
Young.

HIDDEN

There are things in me
That will never thrive here.
There are aspects of me
That cannot grow there.

You think I am a known
Entity.
Because you are familiar with the
Anger,
The patterns of my mother and father–
Watched
The decisions of my siblings, but I am a
Stranger.
What you don't realize is: I am my own
Beast.

Could you even do it?
That thing you make sound so simple.
Could you say goodbye
At the beginning
With just the first taste on your tongue,
The best still yet to come?
Could you swallow that hell,
As I have, with so few complaints?

Now, you want to know
How I am,
But never when you are first
Causing all this pain.
Retroactive is your concern–
When I can no longer tell
What feeling is.

How many of us
Die in pursuit of trying
To just feel alive?

It's been said before–
There are only today's
Never tomorrow's.
I think we must
Have done this to ourselves
On purpose.
What other creatures
Would kill themselves
So slowly
With something just there,
Something always just so
Nonexistent?

They think I cannot see the world is grey—
They forget it is my favorite color.
But to believe that all in existence
Must be that particular shade,
Is to forget that black and white are real,
Are the foundation of even your
Unique blend of the two.

Chaos–
Sweet on my tongue and burning–
The ambrosia of which
I was never meant to indulge.

I am blazing, incandescent with rage–
And I want you to burn too.
I want to leave you with words
That burrow and bite
Beneath your skin
In the same way that my thoughts
Are a hive disturbed
By your careful allusions.
You skirt the issue and speak
So sweetly and prettily.
I would love to shock you,
Would thrive on your chaos,
The dark you pretend away,
Hidden with sad eyes and trembling smiles.
Except–where you couldn't help
But to come at me sideways,
Exposing your whole nature,
I will only ever be direct
Or leave you hanging,
Forever wondering about me.
Because where you must say something,
Anything at all–
Self-control is rarely my issue.

When I say:
I am done with this conversation,
What I really mean
Is that my arms are full,
And I cannot take that
Topic off your hands–
No matter how many times
You try to foist it upon me.
Either take something from me,
Ease these burdens and give
These tired limbs a rest,
Or find someone new
To carry your grocery list
Of grievances.

There's no winning with you!
What you mean, really,
Is that there is no winning against me,
In a fight I wasn't aware of,
On a battlefield I have no wish to be on,
In a war that you alone
Have declared and waged upon us.

I'm filling voids
With my carefully
Thought out
Words.

And you are creating
Them with your
Careless, thoughtless
Screams.

Unfortunately,
Destruction works
So much faster
Than creation can
Sing.

You twirl and sway,
Dancing with a line
That I will not cross,
A line I will carve into granite
To keep myself from
Slipping, too, over the edge.

The lies you have told—
You choose them,
Count each just so,
And try to convince me
That untruths spoken
Only occasionally
Add up to a majority
Of honest living.

Lying to yourself–
It hurts us more than you know.
No space for my truth.

Your words
They hit harder,
Linger longer, and
Keep killing
Well past the last ring
Of your voice
And stroke of your key.

I cannot live in
Artificial peace.
Years under that cold,
Harsh light
Have ruined forever my
False calm.
I need burning sun–
Stinging truth.
Fight for real peace, or
Lose me.

I am water–
Changeable, formless.
I recall being steam,
Remember the chill of ice,
But for now,
I am liquid.
Our relationship is
What you make of it.
If the cup doesn't suit,
Try another,
Or else
Find yourself
A new spring.

You left me
With laughter and pretty words
Tripping off your tongue.
A simple question, and your answer?
Laying the blame that belonged to you,
Sitting in a gilded box at my feet.
A single question, and your answer:
An ornate and useless decree
That shattered my heart–
A blade forged
Of gorgeous destruction.

Waiting–
Curious, anxious eyes on me,
Anticipating the breakdown.
Instead,
I don't stop, can't dwell, though
I wouldn't call it thriving.
Existing,
Perhaps that is a better word:
I am in a perpetual state of
Management.

One clawed inch gained,
Twenty feet slid back,
The sun already over the peak,
The darkness descending–
While you ask for sunsets,
Would expect the rewards
Only earned at the summit.

Trust and respect,
Courtesy and grace:
The things you demand–
The offering you deny.

You want to know my secrets,
See how flawed I am?
You've read my words,
Known my darkness
That I willfully shared unto the world,
And still you think me
Unfeeling and unfathomable.
Am I?
Or are you
Just oblivious to intricacy?

What is a thing without its context?
How can you know a face
From just one angle?
Isn't it strange how quickly
We judge a person,
Based solely on an idea?
The ways in which we conjure
An entire human nature–
Gleaned only from a fragment of their lives.

Why do humans think
That disagreement must mean
Only hate exists?

People may change–
Potential remains the same.

So tired
Of everyone leaving
Their emotions lying
All over the place
And expecting that someone
Will pick up after them.

Sometimes,
I want to stroll past,
To say that I disagree
With your position.
But then I scroll back,
And I give you my heart–
Because I would rather
You look back and see it.
And when you say,
How could you
Endorse
That decision?
I can smile and respond:
What I have always
Supported
Was you.

I would rather create
Thousands of small moments
With you,
Than celebrate only the big ones
For you.

A boundary *is*.
It cannot be
Reconfigured at will.
A fence, a stone wall,
Has no elasticity.
Wood can be changed,
Stone can be moved,
But it is no simple task.
Instead,
The reshaping is accomplished
With effort and work—
Via sweat and strain—
By tearing down what was
And rebuilding as needed.
They are not permanent,
Never made to be fixtures,
Immortal.
But still:
When the reckoning comes,
A boundary
Can only be counted
In one of two ways:
Broken or unbroken?

How to strike the balance
When I believe loving means
Being set free
And you believe it is
A crutch to be wielded.

You poke your mind full of holes,
Trying to make more space for your ideas,
And then wonder why you can no longer
Bear any weight of disagreement,
Hold on to any water or truth.

Tingling pinpricks
On lips
That finally still–
That's what anger
Feels like.

Refusing to run, to take a step,
Because–if I caught my footing–
There's a probability
That I would lose myself
Out amongst the grasses and forests,
And never return.

I stretched out on the carpet,
Speaking into the familiar dark,
Too numb to understand you,
Too full of feeling to be understood.

I curled up on the cold hardwood,
Crying into the new dim,
Too mindless to make myself known,
Too full of thoughts to know myself.

I lay beside you on the worn blankets,
Silent in the harsh light,
Too unsure to make the hard decisions,
Too certain to leave it undecided.

I always do end up on the floor.

Interminable,
When all you can do is done,
And still, you must wait.

I call again, but you can't be bothered
To open your eyes.
Instead, you roll back over,
And I–finally finished–
Softly close the door.

How did it get this bad?
How come you never said?
I simply didn't know
There was another way of living,
Any other way of being.

Mirrors are anathema to me
When my heart is heavy and sick,
Because who wants to see it–
The look of your own pain
Refracted through eyes
So familiar?
Why even
Risk a
Glimpse?

Eyes made beautiful–
Polished into a bright jade
When drowned in the depths.

Trust only
In their eyes–
Abandoned,
One day,
To the pain
In her smile.

My mind is dirty–
Though perhaps not in the way
You might think.
It has endured,
Despite being worn upon
By thoughts with a heavy tread.
Has been dragged through
The muddiest of emotions
And made it–somehow–to the other side.
Bears, even still,
The wounds left by others,
Sliced ragged by their words.
It is bloodied by my own
Careless and reckless treatment.
My mind is still a mess
Because the scars
Are painstaking to heal
And the dirt is difficult
To scour away.

She says to not give the feelings power,
To let every emotion flee and escape your grasp
As soon as its havoc is wrought.
But what is the purpose, the value in that?
How much more do they win over you by being free?
Free to come back as they wish,
Free to haunt your every step,
Free to indulge in your mind and spirit?
No, I do not let them be.
By holding them to me,
By allowing them to dwell within,
I know them better and master even
The most unruly of thoughts,
The darkest of emotions.
Only by binding them to myself do I win.
They can have no mastery over me–
Not while I know where they lie,
How deep their depths plunge,
Am intimate with the shapes of their malice.

I know how it feels
To have someone say–
While looking into your soul–
That they hold in contempt
A core part of you,
Believe at your base you are flawed.
I know the depth,
The shock of that pain,
But I am not broken
By even the opinions of those
I hold closest to my heart.
When there is security within,
Who can assail you from without?
And even still, I can cherish those
Who would find my being invalid.
Because they are not me,
And I am more than one thing.
And even if I wasn't,
I know and am known,
Not misunderstood or discounted by all.
There can be love,
Even in the midst of the greatest,
Gravest, of hurts.

Squeezed,
Encased on all sides,
Pressured into being.
But when gravity has had its say,
When the crushing desists,
I am changed and the same,
Stronger for it.
The weight was not mine,
No choice in it for me,
But even so,
Used to my own advantage until
My true nature was revealed:
Made to burn
And made to shine–
Imperfections and all.

GROWN

I am history,
Living and creating.
I am legacy,
Forging and cultivating.

Seek peace and pursue it.
Did you know–
That they were different,
That the finding
Is just the beginning?

The movies haven't changed,
Just me.
The child who saw
Became the girl who empathized–
Grew into the woman who knew.
And the tears come all the faster
For the lack of imagination,
For the brokenness of experience.

Dismantling what was
To create something *other*.
Because it may not be
Worth keeping the whole,
But–while the bones are still good–
The pieces could be a triumph.

The place between ages,
Something out of the dark, inner being.
Purpose is found
In the need to learn, know, remember.

A smudged circle of light:
The flame
Slowing and flickering,
As focus is found,
Drawn deeper.

Disillusioned, yet–
I am still here, present now–
Hope for what may come.

Maybe I'm so attached
To sleep
Because it is such a powerful
Indicator–
That all is right with a mind,
The soul.
If mine is so troubled, then what
Must I yet face?

The grogginess washed away,
Replaced with surprise.
But was it truly?
A simple phrase,
Then started the change–
As if brought on by the words.

Mired by grief,
Drowning in all the sadness
That finally caught up to me–
But at least you gave me the anger
That allowed me to find the words
That can keep me afloat.

So much baggage
When I thought
I traveled lightly.
I'll unpack it all
Someday.
But for now,
The lot will sit
In its corner
Until–piece by piece–
The job gets done
Eventually.

That place that carried
So much hurt,
That space that brought
Together so many pieces
That name I never spoke
Nor deigned to call it—
The claim I never knew
It had on me.

Memories of the past,
Still a surprise.
A familiar space
With different people,
And yet,
The same feelings
Mix with new hurts.
And it's all a fresh sight.
And it's all just an echo.

Fear, then the response,
We grip tighter and tighter–
Instead, just release.

Valid,
Validating,
Validated:
One hundred times over,
And I'll still doubt–
My mind in a nutshell.

So much was concealed,
Freedom is still nerve-wracking,
Comfort far off yet.

Heart skipping a beat,
Craning to look,
Not daring to be relieved yet.

For some reason that I don't know,
That almost look
Was closer to a reasonable explanation
Than any words.

Time to breathe new life–
You do not build the flames first,
But coax the embers.

I've worked so hard
To stay humble
That I've forgotten
How incredible I can be.
What I knew in my bones
As a child,
What I put into reluctant effect
As a teen,
What I allowed to fade into obscurity
As an adult–
No more.

I know by heart
The connotations of you,
While you are still learning
The definitions of me.

I've always been certain.
Known the limits,
The shape,
Of my soul.
The new terms
That I apply to myself–
The words that frighten you–
Are no world-changing thing
To my mind.
Instead, I now have
The definitions required for others
To finally understand
My enduring surety
Of what makes me,
Me.

There was a time
When I draped myself
In colors I did not feel,
Smiles and laughs flashing
To sell a single thought.
Now, I dress myself
In darkness and shadows,
I hold my tongue and lips still
Until it matters and
I know my own mind.
I now expose all
My light and truths
In ways I could not
While looking like
A pretty lie.

The thing you call
Beauty—
It's true name is
Acquiescence.

Never more myself,
Moments of grace and quiet
Where none were before.

If you're wondering,
I've always been
This way.
If you didn't see it
Before,
Then perhaps it was
A mercy for my growth.

My heart breaks for you,
They murmur.
I can't even imagine–
They cut off.
When you view your ordeals
As simply being life,
As something excessively ordinary,
Then these words,
Meant to comfort, become
Unbearable
In ways that the situation itself
Never felt before.

I don't struggle with believing
There are others out there
Like me.
What I find hard to understand:
I have experiences that are
Unordinary.

I have always known myself,
Perhaps too well.
I do not search the world over,
Trying to find me.
I already am.
And I will continue to change
And then,
Still find that I
Still am me–
Just bigger inside.
I must confess
I only barely keep an eye out
For someone similar
In thought and word and wonder.
Because I know myself,
And I keep good company.

I can't say I've ever been robbed
When I've only ever given freely,
Bestowed intentionally,
Or–at least–never regretted
What you must have needed more,
Whether or not I was in a position
To go without.
Even now, knowing all the ways
In which you have taken
And taken advantage,
The moments and the opportunities
And the memories you have stolen–
I can't find it in myself
To count it all a loss.

If you've already explored
Your darkest depths,
It is hard to shock yourself
When the bad times
Do come.
How can you be surprised,
When you've already
Known, accepted, and named
Each of your demons?

I am not for the faint of heart.
I am dragon, queen, and slayer
At once.
I am not here to save or be saved.
I am here by choice–
And I am not here for you.

Why is it,
That the words we speak *to* ourselves—
Those things we whisper inside our heads—
Are kinder than words that we say
Aloud and *about* ourselves
To anyone who would listen?

I persevered through every trial
By knowing it would end.
I chanted:
I can't,
I can't, Ican't,
Ican'tIcan'tIcan't,
Through each one,
For moments.
But–for eternities longer–
I spoke to myself that
I could.

No experiences are repeatable,
Not in truth.
What we think,
How we come to view things—
It all changes with every
Event,
Whether slight and imperceptible
Or monumental and scarring.
Every moment effects
The next outcome,
And over again:
Until everything must be new,
A first encounter.

Another word—
Only because I had no idea,
But that of holding a hand.

I am closed, at the moment.
But it never fails:
You get me to open up.
To be known–
It's a wonder,
Such a wonder.

Always sat silently by,
Your wordless stares now known
For the grace and patience
I could never hear before
In the quiet tone of your love.

I need more from you.
With others,
I don't crave the face-to-face.
Yet *your* expression and inflection:
My comfort–
Born of bone and blood–
How rare a find.

A gift of a word, a hug,
Something small,
Just for you.
Something that will help.

I live the slow life,
Prefer to take my time,
Think things out.
But I function by multi-tasking.
My replies are compliments and instructions
At once.
My eyes and ears are aware
Of two separate realities.
And, if both my hands
Are tied by one task,
The frustration mounts.
So I stop,
Slow,
Breathe.
One world for sight and sound,
One meaning per comment.
And two hands for each work.

Not my excuse for you,
My grace for myself.

How to balance?
The sense
Of running out
Of time,
With the knowledge
That it's still not
Too late
To start again.

Not yet where I want,
Unsure how to reach that point.
Just keep crawling on.

The reason we're here—
To take our chances,
One at a time.
Wait for the right start.
Ready to say:
I know.

Subdued,
But not tamed.
Coaxed,
But never controlled.

I admire the way
You have broken cycles
And forged new paths
Bravely.

Let me only be settled
Once my life has been lived.
Let nothing fall to the wayside
Until it is complete.

ABOUT THE AUTHOR

Younger is Kiana Lin's fifth full-length work, and she is–of course–still writing! To follow along on her journey and learn more, visit her website: www.creativeinklin.com

Ever since she was a child, Kiana Lin has had a love of words. From her first made up phrase (to fit her stubborn idea) to learning to read (out of a spiteful need for independence), she took in every bit of wordplay and storytelling craft that she could. Then, one summer, a creative writing assignment led to a late brainstorming session in her aunt and uncle's kitchen. That one night sparked the desire to create something she would enjoy reading for herself.

And then she never stopped.

www.ingramcontent.com/pod-product-compliance
Lightning Source LLC
Chambersburg PA
CBHW030302100526
44590CB00012B/488